DOODLE & DECOR

Coloring Book

for Adults
Who Adore Decor

RANIA MOUSA

ISBN-13: 978-1985538191
ISBN-10: 1985538199

This coloring book belongs to the creative

Email **rania_mousa@hotmail.com**
to stay connected for exciting new releases

Try your colors here

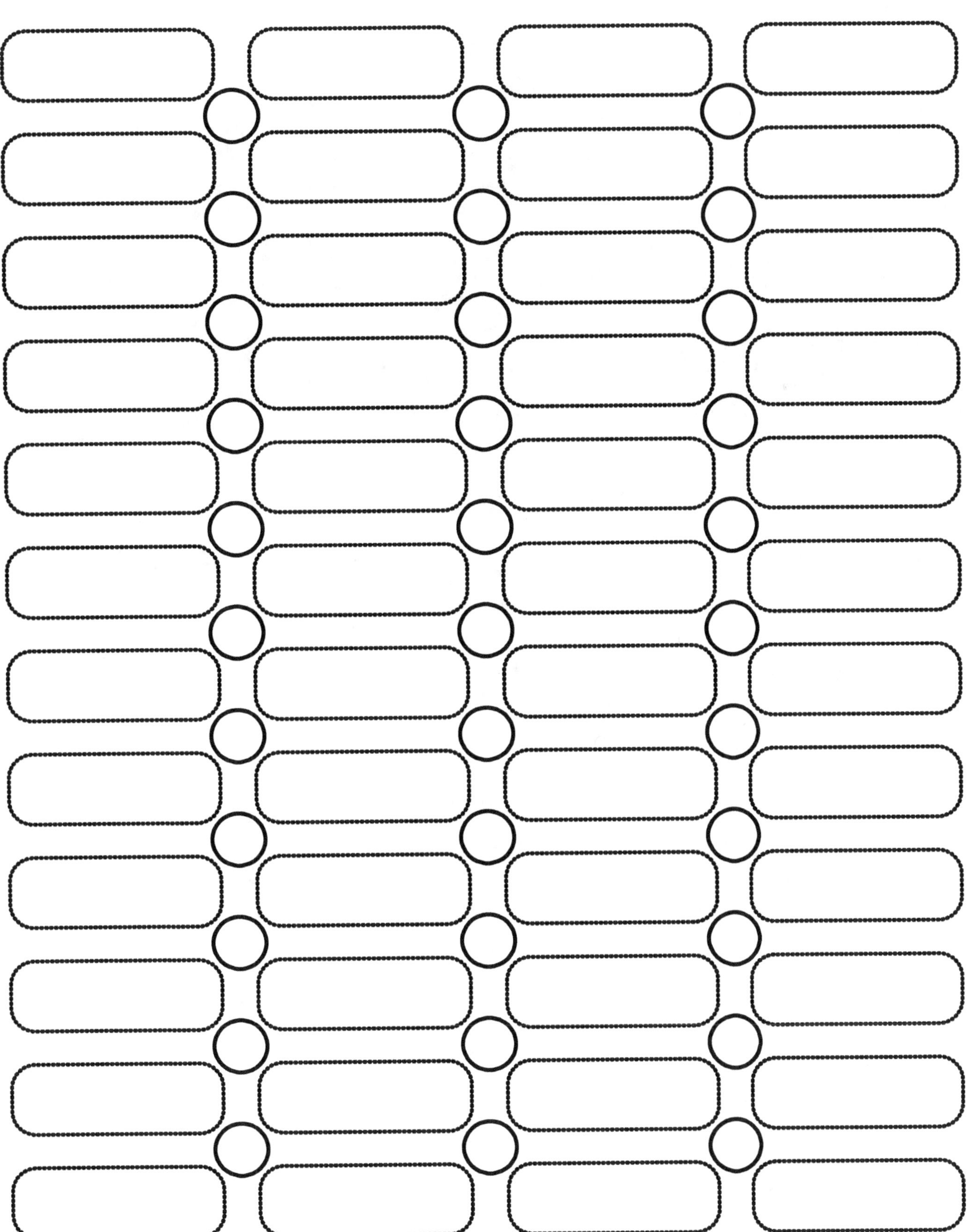

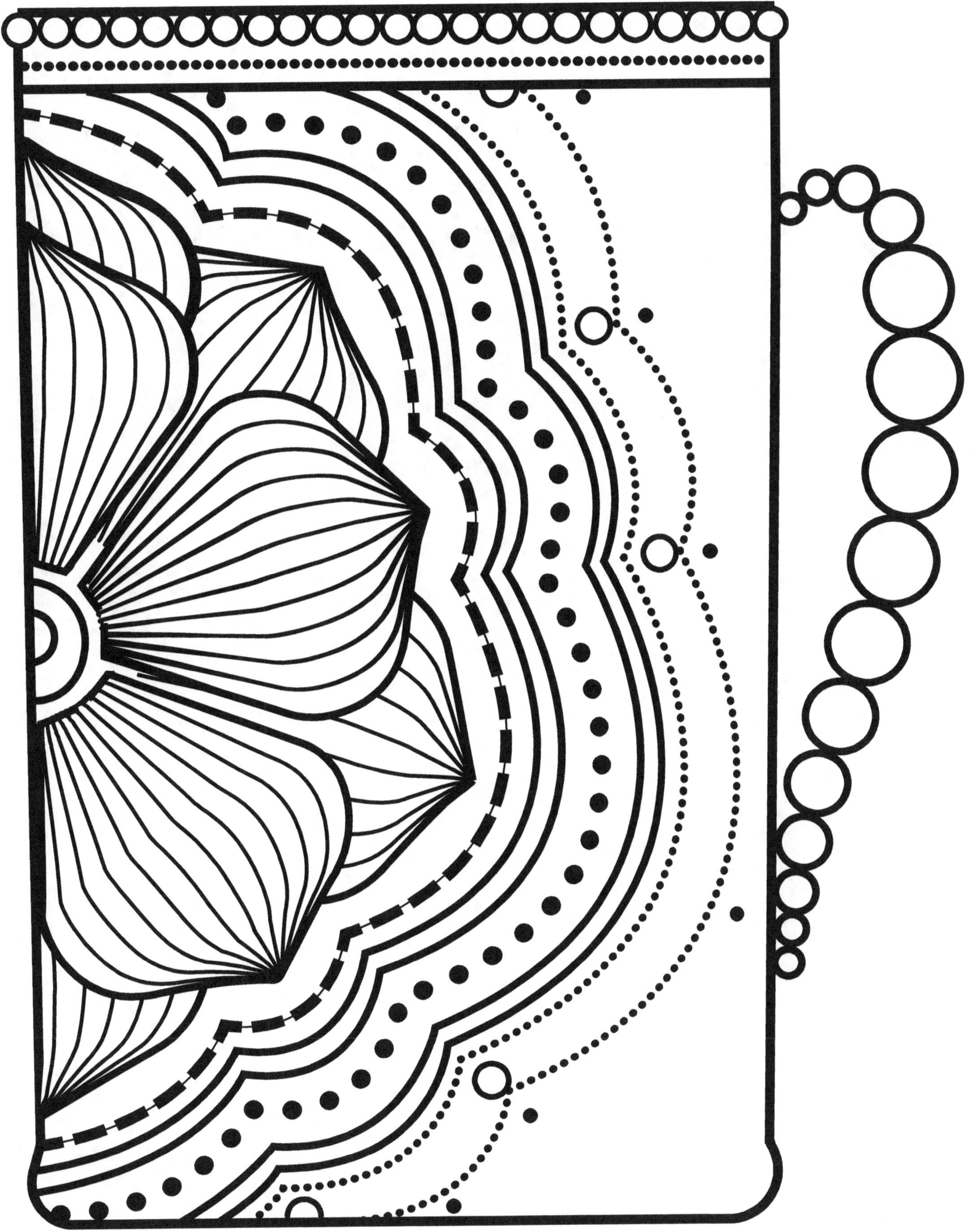

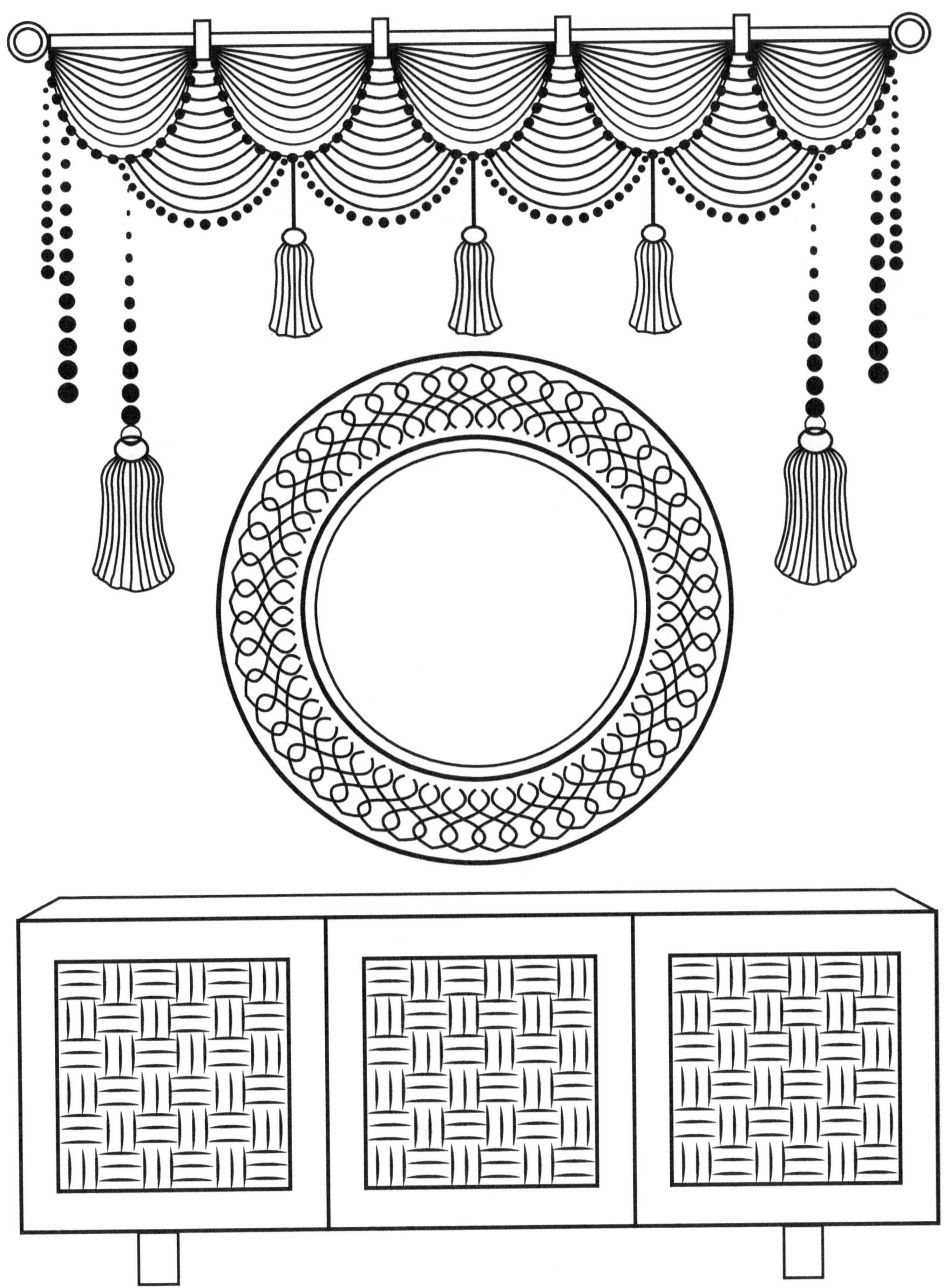

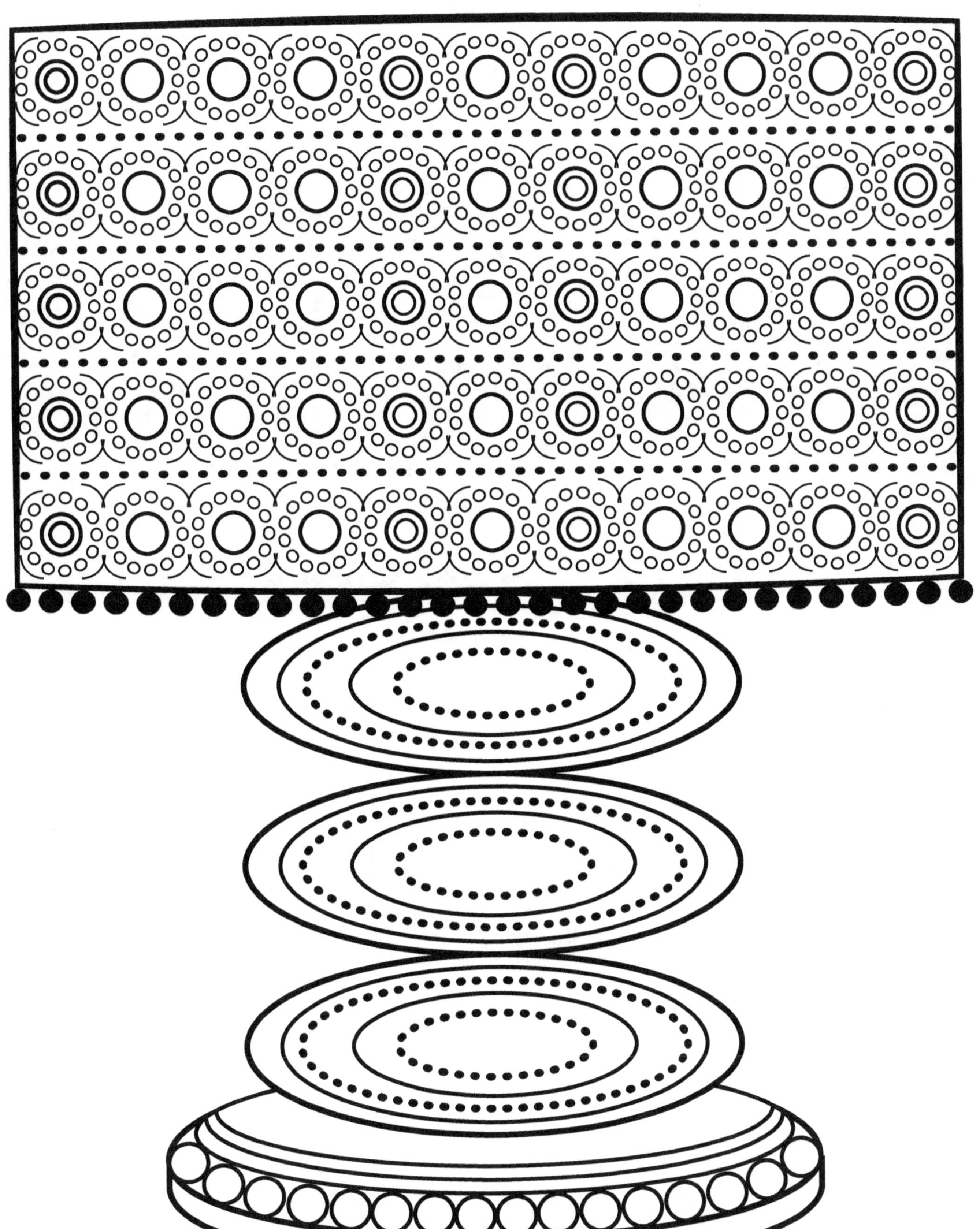

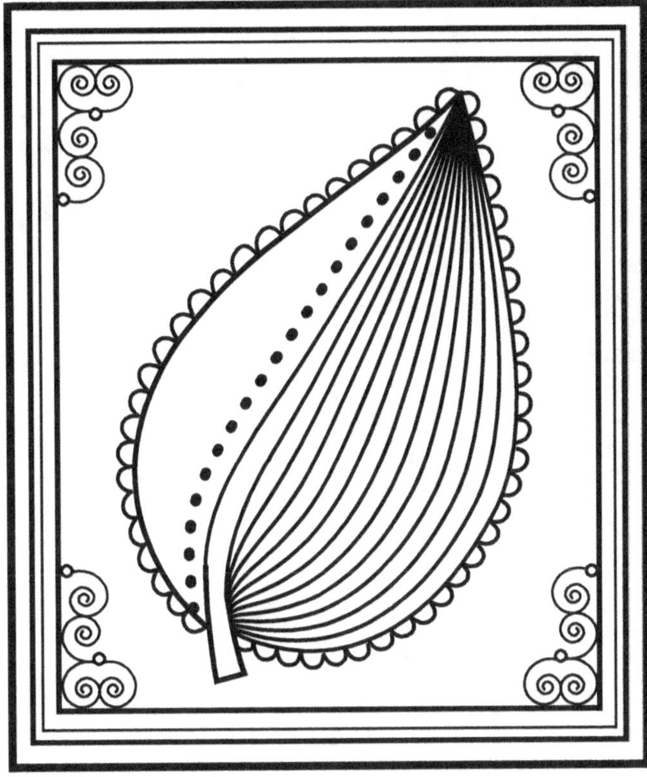

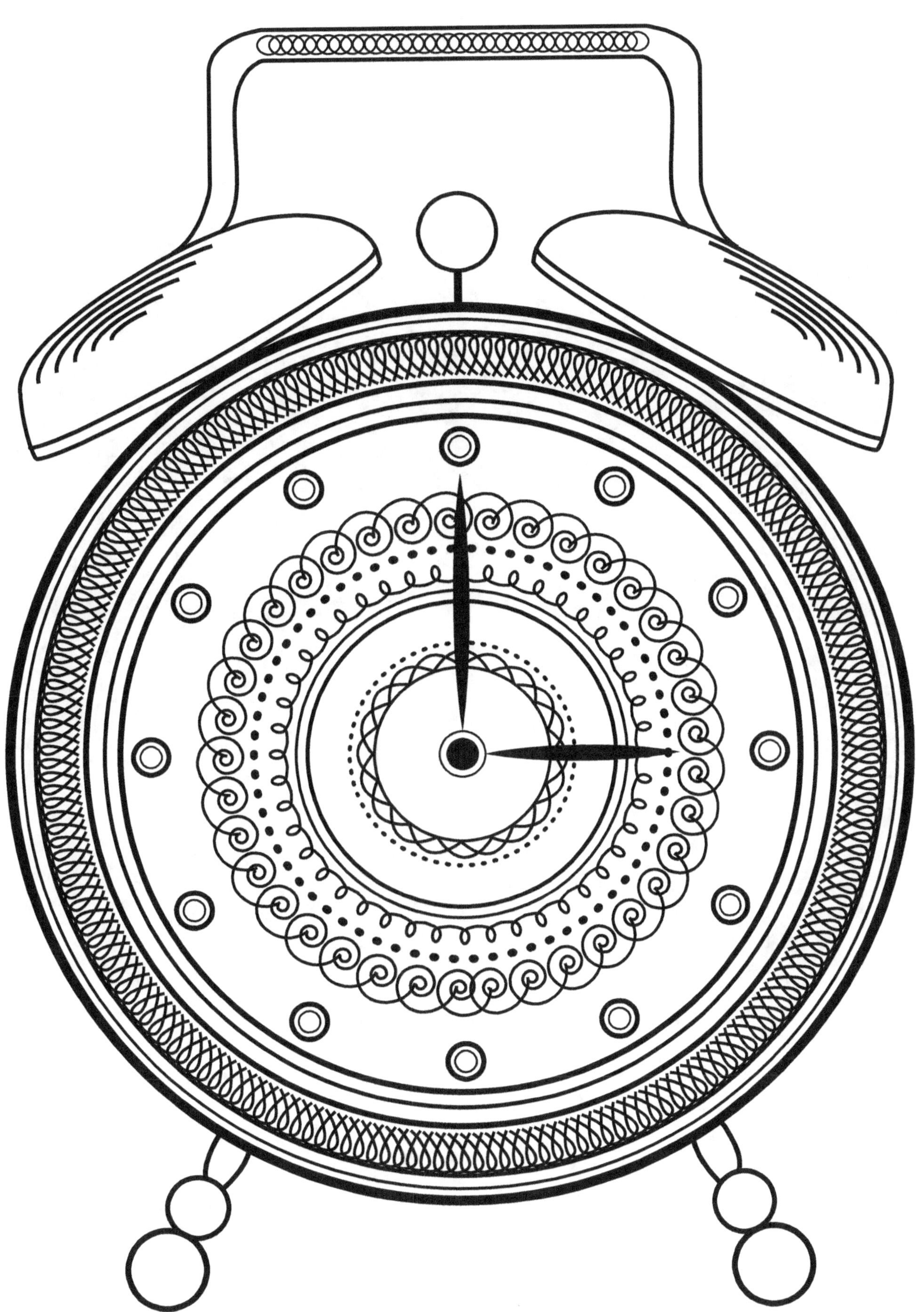

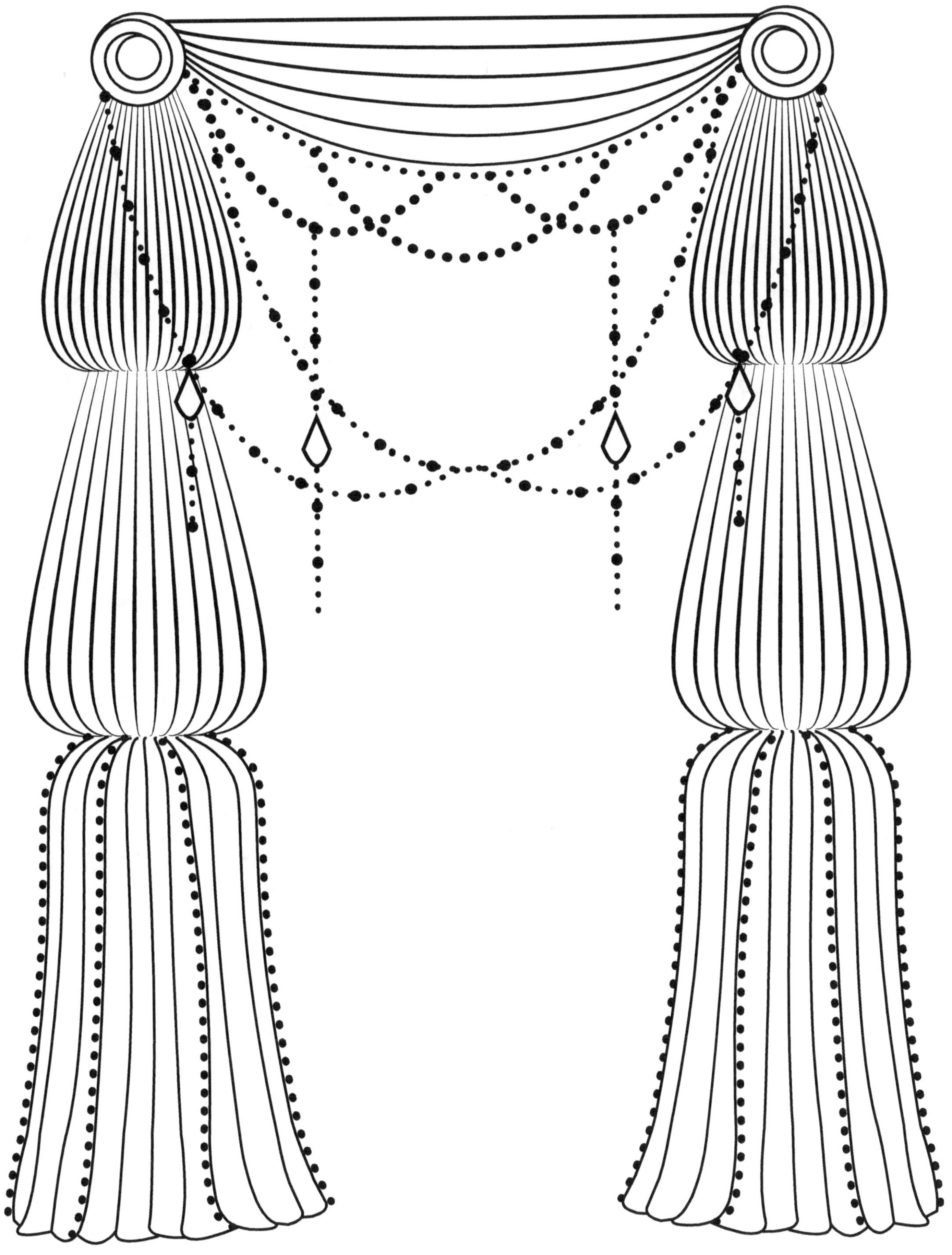

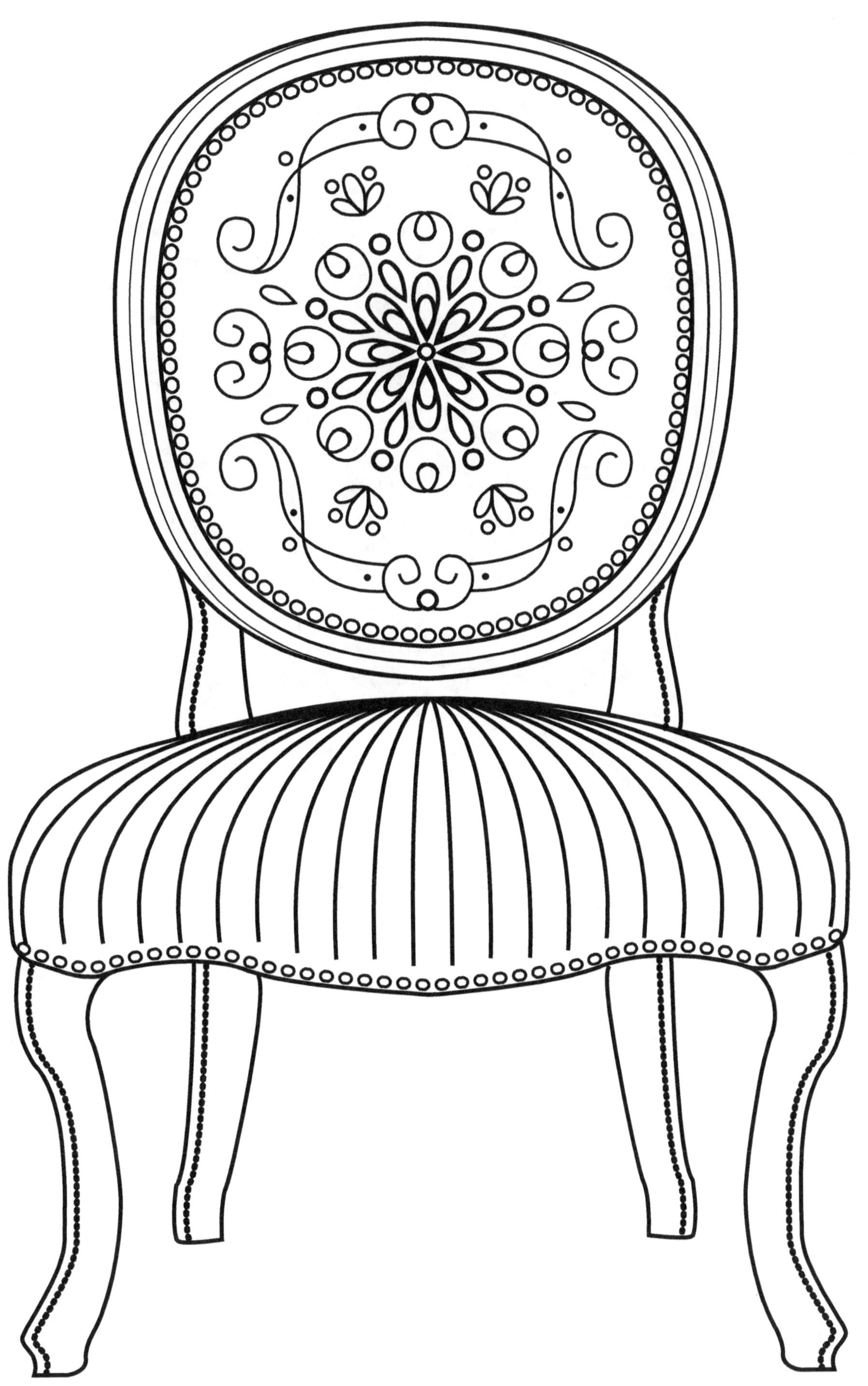

www.ingramcontent.com/pod-product-compliance
Lightning Source LLC
Chambersburg PA
CBHW081851250726
48659CB00008B/2701